History for Kids:
The Renaissance

Contents

Introduction

Following the darker periods of the Middle Ages, the time of rebirth between the 14th century and the 17th century in Europe is known as the Renaissance period. During this time, many great people lived, including scientist and astronomer Galileo Galilei, the artists Michelangelo and Raphael, and the writer Shakespeare. These are only a few of the many incredible people of the Renaissance you can expect to learn about in this book.

As you read, you'll learn about the three notable centuries of the Renaissance period. We can still see many of the influences today, and many pieces of writing and art still exist from that period. The scientific discoveries of then would go on to influence the sciences of today. Many topics will be covered, including:

- The Beginning of the Renaissance
- Major Events of the Renaissance
- Humanism
- Expansion during the Renaissance
- Writers of the Renaissance
- Artists of the Renaissance
- Philosophers and Thinkers of the Renaissance

- Scientists of the Renaissance
- How the Renaissance Influences Our Lives Today

Understanding the Renaissance and what it meant means gaining a greater understanding of human society. The ideas of the Renaissance still exist even centuries later. The liberal arts, sciences, and ideas of the time paved the way for our modern life. These influences are clear across developments in science and technology, the political climate, and focus on the liberal arts.

Hopefully, this book will teach you a little more about the influence of the Renaissance. Happy learning!

Chapter 1: Setting the Tone for the Renaissance

The early years of the Renaissance set the stage for the critical turning point it would be for civilization. It bridged the gap between modern-day civilization and the Middle Ages, being a period of rebirth for most of humanity, and was rich in art, music, and the sciences. Many great thinkers and philosophers emerged during the time, and global exploration was at its peak, inviting the culture of new lands to European commerce.

Though the Middle Ages were considered a darker time, historians generally agree accounts are exaggerated, but had a few advancements in science and art. The fall of the Roman Empire also left many people struggling with war, famine, and plagues like the Black Death that spread across Europe. Times were hard, but they also created the ideal conditions for the impending Renaissance period.

The Renaissance revived more than just classical literature and art forms. The tone for the Renaissance was set through acceptance of change. The ideas of the time encouraged people to explore, both their own talents and the world around them, which was a far cry from the lives people experienced during the Medieval times. As the Renaissance continued so did the many changes. This chapter will go over some of the ways social structure, religion, human thought, and architecture changed in the Renaissance period. We'll also discuss the geography of the Renaissance. These factors and changes all worked together to make the Renaissance the great period in human history it would become.

The Early Renaissance: Florence, Italy

Florence

The Medici family lived and ruled in Florence, Italy, for six decades at the start of the Renaissance period. They were heavy supporters of the humanist movements, which is one reason people consider Florence as the birthplace of the Renaissance. Though there was a renowned interest in creating art, it was not yet a profitable venture. Florence, however, had both many wealthy citizens who had the finances to support new artists and their ventures as well as a rich cultural history perfect for inspiration.

The ideas that sparked the Renaissance spread first to surrounding Italian city-states, including Bologna, Rome, Venice, Ferrara, and Milan. The ideas didn't spread to France until the 15th century, and then to northern and western Europe. The beginning of the Renaissance period was different for each of the countries across Europe.

The Italian City-States

At the time of the Renaissance, the Italian City-States had come out of economic depression and experienced an economic boom as a result. This boom granted these city-states more wealth and power than other cities in Europe. However, each of the city-states was governed separately, with some having elected leaders and others being ruled by a monarchy. These cities often fought each other over resources and territory. Some of the more important city-states included:

- Florence- As the birthplace of the Renaissance, this city-state was one of the wealthiest, boasting early architectural achievements and was a popular choice among artists looking for work at the time. The Medici family ruled until it became a democracy. Florence was also known for being a banking center and for its textile production.
- Rome- The pope ruled over the Roman city-state and the Catholic Church at the beginning of the 1400s. In 1447, Nicholas V began re-building Rome. Under his leadership, Rome began supporting the arts. Michelangelo and Raphael are both well-known for their work done here, especially on the ceiling of the Sistine Chapel and the construction of St. Peter's Basilica.

St. Peter's Basilica

- Milan- Milan did not become wealthy until later in the 1400s because it was in the Middle Age time period until 1450 when the Sforza family ruled. With a new peace with Florence also came a greater interest in the ideas of the Renaissance. Eventually, Milan became well-known for its metalwork, including weapons and suits of armor.

- Naples- Naples controlled most of the southern part of Italy during the Renaissance and was one of the later cities to embrace the Renaissance. The movement took hold in 1443 when Alfonso I conquered the city. It continued to be a patron of the arts, becoming well-known for the invention of the mandolin and the music produced at the time. Spain conquered Naples in 1504. A small city-state named Ferrara was also known for music and theatre.

Mandolins

- Venice- The island city of Venice gained its wealth and reputation by trading with the Far East, bringing silk and spices back to Italy. Its role took a temporary decline when the Ottoman Empire conquered Constantinople. However, it maintained control over the seas east of Italy. Venice is also known for its production of artistic glassware.

Though the city-states did fight among themselves, an eventual peace was treaty signed in

13

1454. Milan, Naples, and Florence signed The Peace of Lodi. With boundaries in place, the treaty kept things peaceful for three decades.

The Renaissance as a Rebirth

The Renaissance was a rebirth of the knowledge, attitudes, and classical learning from the Ancient Greek and Roman times. People studied classical texts and techniques, often with the intention of improving their own situations. An early founder scholar and poet in the Renaissance, a man named Petrarch is among those credited for inspiring this learning. He had a passion for seeking and understanding the ancient texts, insistent that understanding the available manuscripts would bring about civilizing thoughts.

Petrarch

Though people consider the Renaissance a movement of cultural and intellectual proportions, it was also closely linked to politics, society, and discovery. While older practices and thought were brought back to life, these also

15

spurred dynamic change. Explorers sought after new continents, discovered new trade routes, and created more connections with the world.

While this was the most prominent Renaissance, it was not the only Renaissance in European history. The Carolingian Renaissance took place from the eighth to ninth centuries, and the Twelfth Century Renaissance saw the return of Greek philosophy and science. Every Renaissance was a rebirth of classical culture and thought. Though culture and thought had never disappeared entirely, the Renaissance brought them to the forefront once again.

Social Culture of the Early Renaissance

Wealth and status were heavily responsible for an individual's course in life. Prior to the Renaissance, the Black Death had killed millions. Those who had survived had access to the same resources, and many people rose in the social rankings as a result. Fortunately for artists and scholars of the time, people used wealth and culture to reinforce their statuses in society. By supporting these artists and scholars, the newfound wealth of many Europeans funded the cultural revolution.

Even though the Renaissance spread from country to country, the new arts and ideas were similar but unique to different areas. Often, Renaissance ideas tied into the culture of the area. However, they also tied into the core of this period of rebirth and the potential it had for change. It often spread through the teachings of scholars and diplomats, shared among artists, through marriage, trade, and even military invasions. As the Renaissance was something that spread from a central point, each territory had its own Renaissance period.

Historians often disagree about the end of the Renaissance, with some saying it ended in the 1520s and others saying it ended in the 1620s. This disagreement comes from the spread of the Renaissance, as many European countries experienced it during different time periods. It also spread beyond the borders of Europe and influenced cultures around the world. As it happened at so many different times in different areas, the Renaissance is sometimes broken into geographical groups, including the Italian Renaissance, the English Renaissance, and the Northern Renaissance. It also expanded to the east, Africa, and the Americas.

Religion in the Early Renaissance

The Black Death that had killed millions left many Europeans in fear of an angry, vengeful God. The Black Death reached Europe in the 1350s. People were shocked when large ships carried dead or near-dead sailors into port. Many people expected to see their family again, however, they would find that their family members were deceased or had fallen ill.

Some people isolated themselves from those family members, while others tried their best to care for them. Those infected with the Black Death rarely recovered. The situation was worse because of the nature of the disease. It was airborne, which meant that someone contracted the disease by breathing in infected air.

The poor response to the Black Death was brought about by a lack of understanding about the nature of the disease. People did not understand how it spread and believed God was punishing them. Because of this fear, people of lower social status, wrongdoers, and slaves were often beaten. This type of sacrifice showed the vengeful God that people believed humankind was repenting for its sins.

Though the beatings had nothing to do with its eradication, the Black Death eventually died out. Europe was one of the last areas infected. Looking at the response to the Black Death, the shift in attitude following its eradication marked a major milestone for the Renaissance period. Humanism played a major part in this shift away from religion. Humanism, by definition, is a focus on the human rather than a deity. This shift did not completely eradicate religion—it was still prominent in many people's lives. However, people started to question their own existences and capabilities in a way that led them to separate themselves from religion and celebrate their own strengths. Through embracing these ideas, humanism changed how people looked at religion in their lives. They weren't less moral or ethical in any way. If anything, people had accepted more responsibility for choosing their lives and decisions.

Early in the Renaissance, the Catholic Church was supreme. Christianity was the main religion, and those who did not practice it were often outcasts. However, the Renaissance brought about a change. In addition to the ideas of humanism, the Catholic Church faced challenges from Protestantism. Though Protestantism was a form of Christianity, it still challenged some of the Catholic ideas of the time.

Architecture in the Renaissance

During the Medieval times, people put a good deal of focus on religion and political structure. Much of the architecture attributed to that time is Gothic-style castles and churches. These have a more 'square-like' design toward the top and have even lines.

Notre Dame in Paris is an example of medieval architecture

During the Renaissance, however, architecture changed to reflect the styles of Ancient Rome and Greece. Some features of Renaissance buildings included:

- Square design overall- Though the tops of buildings were rounded, buildings as a whole were constructed from rectangle or square symmetrical shapes.
- Front- The 'façade,' or front, of buildings also had symmetry, usually across a vertical axis, meaning the left side was the same as the right.
- Columns- Columns used during the Renaissance period are similar to those used during the times of the Roman empire.
- Domes and Arches- Greek and Roman architecture inspired the rounded design of building tops.
- Ceilings- During the Middle Ages, ceilings sometimes were left completely open. Renaissance builders generally created flat ceilings, with the exception being the domed areas of buildings.

Though many architectural designs were borrowed from the Greeks and Romans, the man credited with bringing them to life was Filippo Brunelleschi. Considered the first Renaissance architect, Brunelleschi started his first piece of Renaissance architecture in 1419 when he designed the dome that stands above the cathedral of Florence. Many historians also consider this year as the very start of the Renaissance period.

Cathedral of Florence

People consider The Pantheon in Ancient Rome as the largest dome structure, built 1500 years before Brunelleschi's work on the cathedral of Florence. The cathedral's dome was a remarkable piece for its size. This undertaking would take Brunelleschi much of his life to complete. Four million bricks make up the dome, and the gold ball that sits on top weighs almost two tons. To build this, Brunelleschi had to come up with ways to lift the heavy objects high into the air. Other buildings he designed include the churches of Santo Spirito and San Lorenzo.

San Spirito

Many other European churches were designed in a similar style. Some other buildings that have a true Renaissance architectural design include El Escorial, The Sistine Chapel, Basilica of St. Peter, Palazzo Farnese, Pazzi Chapel, and Palazzo Pitti.

El Escorial

The Life of the Average Person During the Renaissance

In the Middle Ages, those of high social status or royalty were more likely to experience the luxuries of life. The average person, or 'peasant,' may have struggled to find food. Even farmers and those who processed goods often had trouble enjoying the fruits of their labors, as those of higher social status taxed goods or took them for their own. While the life of the average peasant or farmer did not change drastically with the Renaissance, they were able to live comfortably. They were able to eat and maintain their lifestyles. However, most still worked from sun up to sun down. The average poor farmer lived in a single-room hut with his family. The average person survived on bread and stew made from whatever was available at the time, usually vegetables or eggs. When possible, the poor would drink wine or beer with their food. Water was not sanitized, so drinking it could cause illness.

Farmers and peasants rarely ate meat. Those near the coast could take advantage of their location by fishing, but most meat was expensive and hard to come by. There was no refrigeration then, so people used salt to preserve meat. As salt was rare, preserved meats were expensive. In addition to stew and bread, people would eat mush, generally oats or wheat soaked in water to soften.

The Lifestyle of the Middle Class

Some peasants and farmers secured a higher social status in the Renaissance. Those with enough wealth to be considered middle-class citizens lived in bigger homes. Compared to the living style that most people are used to today, these homes were dark and cold. The lack of hygiene at the time meant they were likely smelly, too. Technology had not yet developed enough to allow people to have running water or indoor bathrooms. However, middle class had access to many luxuries. Women wore long, fancy gowns while men typically wore pants with a tight coat called a doublet.

Renaissance Fashion

The wealthy had access to food better than just bread and stew. Often, the wealthy hosted huge feasts with many exotic dishes. Though they also ate stew and broth, exotic spices or sugar, secured through trade, flavored the food of the wealthy. Large roasts of pig beef or stag were prepared by boiling and basting with rose water and the juices of the meats. They also ate large game birds, including cranes, peacocks, and swans on special occasions like festivals or weddings. Once the birds were cooked, people used the feathers as decoration. Mutton, pheasant, ham, turkey, chicken, rabbit, and venison were also commonly eaten. Dessert was a 'fruit course' that consisted of jellies, fruit, cheese, and nuts.

Children During the Renaissance

The life you live today is probably vastly different from the lives of children in the Renaissance. Adults expected kids to act maturely. Once kids were old enough, they spoke, acted, and dressed like adults. Most children began working as soon as they were able. Unfortunately, many children grew up feeling unloved by their parents. They worked long hours and did not have time for play. Additionally, most children were not coddled, hugged, or otherwise shown love.

The Renaissance period did bring about a change for children of wealthier families. Children of families with greater status had more free time. They could enjoy their childhood and played instead of worked. Once these wealthier children were older, males were typically sent to college or had a private tutor. Arithmetic and grammar were a heavy focus. After humanism was introduced, some studied public speaking, philosophy, and Latin.

Government During the Renaissance

During the Renaissance, many areas of life underwent radical changes. For many governments, however, the same absolute monarchy system existed as it did during the Middle Ages. Having a single ruler made things simpler during this time. However, war was less of a focus during the Renaissance. Eventually, some areas even evolved to support a democracy.

Florence, Italy, was one area that supported democracy. Wealthy families ruled in accordance with what the people wanted at the time. However, many others ruled without any constraints. Queen Isabella I and her husband Ferdinand II ruled over Spain, and their word was law. Their great-grandson, Philip II, was one of the first in Spain to face struggles, as opposing parties rose up to challenge his laws.

Queen Isabella I

England had a different system, with Elizabeth I ruling alongside a parliament. Even with the parliament, Elizabeth made most of the decisions. In Germany, the Holy Roman Empire still ruled. This setup complicated things, as there was a single emperor at the top who ruled with seven elected officials, many princes, and leaders of the 80 imperial free cities the Holy Roman Empire controlled.

Elizabeth I

Economy

Early in the Renaissance, the economy was poor. Many people fled cities when the Black Death took hold. Any merchants or traders who stayed behind would likely be infected. Even if they were not, all those who had fled had taken their need for goods with them. An economic depression resulted. This depression significantly changed once the Black Death was finally eradicated. As populations began to grow again, a new middle class emerged. Once again, goods and services could be traded and the economy boomed as a result.

As there was not a central power during the Renaissance, the currency was difficult to regulate. Larger towns had a marketplace where people would visit when they needed goods. In smaller towns, craftsmen and merchants would come into town on specific days. Most major cities had their own form of currency. Unfortunately, the value of these coins frequently fluctuated, so it was hard to manage money.

Global Exploration

One positive result of the Middle Ages was that people developed tools for exploration. The original magnetic compass that helped traders find new areas had its flaws but was improved. The astrolabe was also developed during the Middle Ages and used for Renaissance exploration. Explorers used astrolabes to measure the distance of the sun and stars from the horizon helping them find their latitude and location.

Astrolabe

Many areas of the world had already been explored. Portuguese cartographers made maps during the time. Travelers and explorers would give them information when they traveled, and cartographers would record it. Ships made further trade and exploration possible. Rather than relying on people to push boats using oars, ships used sails, making for bigger boats and more efficient travel.

All these factors came together to encourage trade. During the Renaissance, many roads traversed the European continent. However, this network of roads was confusing and poorly maintained. When the roads were good, thieves could easily steal from traders, which made sailing a better alternative for trading. Additionally, as the economy boomed, imported goods were in higher demand.

The most popular trading locale outside of the European continent was Asia. In Asia, traders could get the spices, such as cinnamon, mace, peppercorns, and nutmeg, they needed for luxury foods. The East also provided luxury items including fine silk and precious gems. While most traders could not afford to take to the seas on their own, investors would pay the traders and sell the goods for profit.

Chapter 2: Great Artists and Art of the Renaissance

We know about many great Renaissance artists today. Some experienced fame in their lifetime, while others would not become famous until they had passed, and their art was discovered centuries later. Many paintings and sculptures from this time period can be seen in museums across the world. The information available on many of these artists comes from the book, *Lives of the Most Eminent Painters, Sculptors, & Architects* by Giorgio Vasari. He was in the social circle of many of these artists, though he never achieved fame as an artist himself. Published in 1568, the book documented the lives and works of many later Renaissance artists. The other information available has been pieced together from available documents and surviving paintings from the time.

Donatello (Donato di Niccolo di Betto Bardi)

Statue of Donatello in Florence, Italy

Born in Florence in 1386, Donatello was one of the older Renaissance painters and had close ties to the Medici family. Donatello likely received his earliest training from a local goldsmith. He began apprenticing under sculptor and metal smith, Lorenzo Ghiberti, in 1403. Donatello also worked closely with Ghiberti in creating the bronze doors at the Baptistery of the Florence Cathedral.

Detail photo of The Gates of Paradise by Lorenzo Ghiberti, made in 1452

Sometime around 1407, Donatello became friends with once rival-artist Filippo Brunelleschi. They traveled to Rome together, and the two might have studied the ruins of classical Rome. These classical influences and Brunelleschi's Gothic style are apparent in some of Donatello's earlier pieces.

Donatello's Art

Following the learning period of his life, Donatello went on to create many pieces of art. His rendition of the *David* was a life-size statue carved from marble. The Gothic style he learned is clear in the expressionless face and long, graceful lines. This style was quite emotionless compared to Donatello's later work.

Donatello worked with Italian architect and sculptor Michelozzo around 1425. As both had studied alongside Lorenzo Ghiberti, the pair worked well together. They were commissioned to create several architectural-sculptural tombs. Their work would inspire many future Florentine burial chambers. Among the tombs they created were those for Cardinal Brancacci and Antipope John XXII.

Donatello's second depiction of *David* was much more well-known than his first. This sculpture was commissioned by Cosimo de Medici. This time, the sculpture was created from bronze and stands free of any architectural surroundings. The message sent by *David* is one of the triumph of civic virtue over irrationality and brutality, which aligned closely with the ideals of the time.

Drawing of statue of David by Donatello

Another of Donatello's famous bronze statues was *Gattamelata*. Created in Padua, mercenary Erasmo da Narni commissioned this piece.. The statue shows the mercenary riding a horse, dressed as if he were ready for battle. This piece was incredibly controversial at the time as only kings and rulers were depicted on equestrian statues. Despite its controversial nature, the statue went on to inspire many others that followed.

Gattamelata

Crucifixion was another of Donatello's notable pieces. Though it was a bronze relief sculpture, it mimicked a painting with its depiction of a scene and attention to detail. It was made using bronze, gold, and silver around 1465. Its unique design creates a play of light and darkness with the shadows across the surface of the sculpture.

Sandro Botticelli (Alessandro di Mariano Filipepi)

Botticelli was born in 1455 in Florence. Though he was born early in the Renaissance, his painting style in his works including the *Primavera* and *The Birth of Venus* capture the true Renaissance spirit. He was named Botticelli, or 'little barrel' after a nickname given to his brother who worked as a pawnbroker. He was especially skilled in the arts of fresco and panel painting. His linear perspective also allowed him to achieve a sense of human symmetry and perfection in his works, which is especially clear in *The Birth of Venus*.

Botticelli studied under Filippo Lippi, one of the most respected Florentine masters whose style was much softer and more delicate than what Botticelli's style would become, for several years. While Filippo Lippi's impacts can be clearly seen in Botticelli's choice of paler colors and delicate, fanciful dress, the student developed stronger lines and more resonant color schemes.

In addition to what he learned from Lippi, Botticelli also studied the sculptural aspects under

Andrea del Verrocchio and Antonio Pollaiuolo, two notable painters. In 1482, he contributed to the Sistine Chapel.

Andrea del Verrocchio

Botticelli's Art

Botticelli painted *The Birth of Venus,* commissioned by Medici, in 1485. Though Venus is considered a mythological goddess, the idea was to depict a singular event rather than to tell a mythological story. It is part of a collection, with the paintings *Primavera*, *Pallas*, and *Venus and Mars.*

Botticelli created *Virgin and Child with an Angel* sometime before 1740. In this picture, Botticelli shows a mother and child embracing with an angel nearby. This work is one of several by Botticelli with a similar style. There is a painting of the Virgin Mary and her baby without an angel, as well as a version with two angels instead of one.

Hieronymus Bosch

Hieronymus Bosch is known as being one of the major artists from outside Italy that followed a humanist approach. He was most well-known in the countries of the Netherlands, Spain, and Austria. Bosch lived from 1450 to 1516, and he probably learned to paint from his family, as his father was an artistic adviser and his grandfather and uncles worked as artists.

Bosch's most well-known painting is *The Garden of Earthly Delights*, which historians believe was created between 1495 and 1505. This unique piece is a triptych, which is a painting with three panels hinged together. On the left, God is introducing Adam and Eve to the Garden of Eden. The middle panel displays the temptations of society, and the right panel depicts Judgment Day. Art scholars believe the underlying theme of this piece may have been the dangers of temptation.

Example of a triptych

Leonardo da Vinci

Leonardo da Vinci

Da Vinci is arguably one of the most famous artists from the Renaissance. He is less-known for his inventions but became an incredibly famous painter. Da Vinci was born in 1452 and studied art for four years from 1466 beginning as an apprentice. It took him a few years to showcase his abilities, but he started accepting commissions in 1478. Da Vinci's art projects of the time ranged from designing monuments to helping with parade floats.

Regarding his art, there are only about 15 of his paintings that still survive. There were many pieces that da Vinci did not finish before his death in 1519, as he frequently tried new techniques (and without success). Da Vinci was also known for his procrastinating attitude, mainly because he studied so many fields. However, the drawings, concepts, and scientific diagrams in his sketchbooks would go on to contribute to many different fields.

Da Vinci's Art

Though the *Mona Lisa* depicts what looks like a woman, some historians believe that it may have been a self-portrait of da Vinci. Other theories are that the *Mona Lisa* was a portrait of a citizen's wife. Da Vinci painted the *Mona Lisa* between 1503 and 1506. Today, you can see it in Paris, France, at the Louvre Museum.

Mona Lisa

The Last Supper is an iconic painting of Jesus and his twelve disciples, at the time when Jesus knew that one would betray him. This painting was a mural constructed between 1495 and 1497 that covers a monastery wall in Milan, Italy. However, because of the way da Vinci experimented with oil and tempera paint on the drywall, the modern-day mural is mostly a reconstruction that has been maintained and restored over time.

The Last Supper

Vitruvian Man is a painting of a man superimposed in two positions. It is named after the architect Vitruvius. People believe da Vinci created it in 1490. The drawing is located in Venice, Italy at the Gallerie dell'Academia, however, it is not permanently displayed.

Vitruvian Man

Albrecht Durer

Albrecht Dürer Self Portrait

Born in 1471 in the city of Nurnberg, Germany, Durer is one of the most influential artist of the German Renaissance. Many of his art pieces were religious in nature. He had a Gothic style apparent in his earlier work and was most well known for his religious works, altarpieces, and copper engravings. He also did several portraits and self-portraits, as well as woodcuts.

Before he was trained as a painter, Durer worked in his father's goldsmith workshop. However, he was only 13 when he completed his first self-portrait and 14 when he completed the painting *Madonna with Musical Angels*. Recognizing his obvious talent, his father secured Durer an apprenticeship with Michael Wohlgemuth, a woodcut illustrator and painter of the time.

Durer would visit Italy for the first time around 1494. Here, he learned many new painting techniques from the Renaissance artists of the time, which are apparent in his later works. Some of his early influences include Andrea Mantegna, Antonio Pollaiuolo, and Giovanni Bellini.

One of the last and greatest painting Durer created was *The Four Apostles*. Completed in 1526, the painting depicts Saints John, Peter, Paul, and Mark. Artists celebrate his work as some of the most beautiful pieces of art across the European continent. Dürer would influence Dutch, Italian, German, and other artists.

Michelangelo Buonarroti

Michelangelo Buonarroti

Though this iconic artist was born in Caprese, Italy in 1475, he grew up in Florence. Michelangelo holds the titles of painter, sculptor, and architect. He got his start young, being invited to live at the palace of Lorenzo de' Medici and began his apprenticeship at age 13-14. He worked with many people in Medici's social circle and was eventually commissioned by many notable works during the Renaissance, including a cathedral, a cardinal, and the pope.

Lorenzo de' Medici

Michelangelo is one of the most well-documented artists of his time. While others would achieve later fame, he was in high demand during his lifetime. Many of his pieces depicted perfectionism and incredible attention to detail. While Michelangelo insisted his ideas were his own and that he created art without outside influence, some of his Madonna pieces show obvious influence from the work of Leonardo da Vinci.

Michelangelo's Art

David symbolizes the ideal of human perfection during the Renaissance. Incredible attention to detail went into this statue, which stands 17-feet tall. The *David* was commissioned in 1501 and was modeled after the biblical hero.

Head of the statue David

The Pope commissioned the ceiling of the Sistine Chapel in 1508, and it took Michelangelo four years to complete. While Michelangelo was originally paid to depict the twelve apostles, he painted nine scenes from the Book of Genesis in the Bible. Within these nine scenes, there were seven male prophets and five female prophets. The most famous scene depicted was *The Creation of Adam*, a piece where God reaches out to Adam and they touch hands.

Illustration of The Creation of Adam

Michelangelo had many other famous art pieces in his time that can be found all around Europe. They are dispersed because, like many other artists, he sought out work in cities beyond Italy, especially following the fall of the Medici family in 1494. Some of his pieces include:

- The Tomb and Shrine of St. Dominic-Michelangelo completed this piece in Bologna. It was the work by a deceased sculptor that had not been finished. Michelangelo carved the last of the small figures that completed the tomb and shrine. His three figures stood out more than the previous sculptures because of his attention to detail.

- The Bacchus- Designed between 1496 and 1497, the Bacchus is one of Michelangelo's first sculptures, depicting the Roman God of Wine, Bacchus. The pose of Bacchus suggests drunkenness depicted by a staggering body and rolling eyes.

- The Pietà- The Pieta is the only sculpture Michelangelo ever signed. It was created between 1498 and 1499 using Carrara marble. In this art, the body of Jesus is lying across his mother's, Mary, lap following the crucifixion. It was originally created for Cardinal Jean de Bilheres' funeral and was later moved to St. Peter's Basilica.

The Pieta

Raphael (Raffaello Santi)

Postage stamp with image of Raphael

Though Raphael only lived 37 years, his classical painting techniques would continue to influence artists well into the middle of the nineteenth century. He was influences by arts by Uccello, Mantegna, Piero Della Francesca, and Perugino, though he likely received training from his father, who was a court painter, as well. Raphael was born in 1483 and became most well-known during his lifetime for creating portraits and paintings of Madonnas.

Raphael's good connections were also improved by his family's wealth. He served as an apprentice under Pietro Perugino for four years beginning in 1500. Raphael would go on to be commissioned for many paintings in his lifetime, as his high social status gave him connections to the people who would pay for his art.

While his social circle attracted those who praised Raphael's great works, it also attracted enemies. Raphael is considered one of the most diverse painters of the Renaissance period because he was incredibly talented at absorbing and learning the styles of those around him. There were obvious influences from other artists, and Raphael had taken to these styles naturally. Michelangelo even accused him of plagiarism, though his accusations were never proved.

Raphael's Art

Postage stamp depicting Sistine Madonna

The *Sistine Madonna* is one of Raphael's most
analyzed pieces. The way it is painted shows clear
influence from Perugino. Painted in the early

1500s, the Madonna may have been a depiction of Raphael's mistress, who he was with from 1508 until his death in 1520.

Saint George and the Dragon is one of two pieces by Raphael with a similar theme. It was a painting within a series of mini panels that was painted in Florence in celebration for the court of Urbino. The painting told the story of Saint George, a Roman soldier of Christian faith. He killed a dragon that had followed the daughter of a pagan king into a city, which then prompted the king and all those who followed him to become Christians.

Raphael moved to work in the Vatican in Rome in 1508 and Pope Julius II commissioned Raphael to paint his private library. Here, Raphael completed different works that had been commissioned by a predecessor. As a whole, the work done in the library is called *Stanza della Segnatura*. Several individual pieces were painted on each of the walls, including *The Disputation of the Holy Sacrament*, *The School of Athens*, and *Parnassus*.

Titian (Tiziano Vecelli)

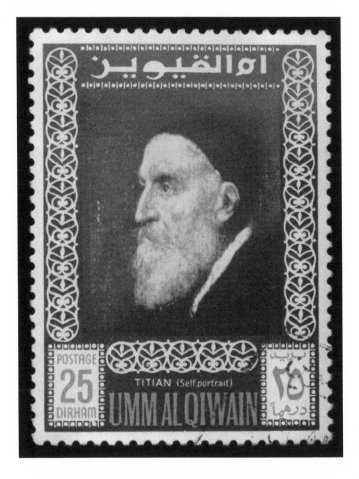

Postage stamp with image of Titian self-portrait

Historians argue the date of Titian's birth even though it is officially recorded as 1477. Many historians believe Titian was born in the mountain village of Pieve di Cadore on a mountaintop in Italy between 1488 and 1490. He received his schooling at the Venetian School of Art, and is considered the greatest Renaissance painter who graduated from here. His great attention to emotion and the idea of human perfection are depicted across his art. Titian would have his works recreated by famous masters like Nicolas Poussin and Rubens, who complimented him in their imitation of his style.

He received his training early, traveling to Venice with his brother at the age of nine. There, Titian would live with his uncle and study under Sebastiano Zuccato, who was known for his work with mosaics. Then, he studied under Giovanni Bellini, who was considered the most talented Venetian painter at the time. Titian worked so closely with Bellini that their styles were very similar, and they collaborated on projects like the frescoes of the Fondaco dei Tedeschi.

Titian's Art

Though Biblical art was popular at the time, Titian was poetic with many of his pieces. He did have some religious themes, but he is also known for telling a story through his work.

One of Titian's religious paintings, *Assumption*, was created between 1516 and 1518. This work makes a profound statement about the Virgin Mary and her triumph as she ascends and can be found in Venice at the high altar of Santa Maria dei Frari. The position of the Madonna in this painting shows influence from Michelangelo and Raphael.

Assumption by Titian

Bacchus and Ariadne is one part of a series that Titian and other Renaissance artists, including Dosso Dossi and Bellini, painted. The Duke of Ferrara commissioned the artists to paint murals on the walls of the Alabaster Room in the Ducal Palace. This painting shows the God of Wine, Bacchus, as he jumps from his chariot upon seeing Ariadne on the Greek island Naxos. It shows the story of a classical piece of literature by Ovid and Catullus. Classical literature was a common theme in Titian's work.

Venus and Adonis is an image that has been painted and re-painted many times. So many versions of this original painting exist that it is hard to tell if the original survived. It illustrates the story of the maiden Venus who is hit by Cupid's arrow and falls for Adonis. Adonis later befalls a tragic fate, and she cannot save him. The version credited to Titian was painted in 1554, and is the 'Prado' version of this painting, meaning it features three dogs instead of two. Though this painting was from 1554, people believed it is a rendition of another painting done by Titian in the 1520s.

While the Renaissance period was a time for creative expression, nothing has quite captured the spirit like art pieces from that era. Many of these pieces are still displayed in museums or owned by private collectors. Others have been refurbished or recreated. These paintings, sculptures, and murals speak of the true Renaissance spirit. They promote respect of the church and appreciation of the classics. Others capture the idea of human perfection and achievement in the era.

Chapter 3: Renaissance Entertainment

The Renaissance period had a lot more middle-class citizens than the Middle Ages did. These people did not have to toil all day and night as farmers and peasants previously did to earn a living and maintain their lifestyles leaving plenty of time for entertainment. Entertainment during the Renaissance period included music, dancing, and theatre. The invention of the printing press allowed people greater access to music and plays than before because composers could share their ideas with those who knew how to play instruments. Several musical instruments were also invented and used during the Renaissance period, including the violin.

Music and Dance

Music and dance were among the best forms of entertainment, as they did not cost anything. Even farmers and peasants could sing and dance for enjoyment. As the Renaissance continued, people began learning new combinations of voices and how to play instruments. Many famous composers also lived during this time, including Thomas Tallis, Josquin Des Prez, and William

Byrd. In 1607, Claudio Monteverdi wrote the first dramatic opera.

Vocal Music

One popular form of music at the time was choir music. It became popular in the church, where different vocals and voice types were woven together to produce a unique melodious harmony. The interweaving method became known as polyphony. Madrigal, a type of vocal music that had at least 3-6 singers, also became popular. Several melodies were sung at once to create a greater sense of emotion. Romantic poems were commonly sung as madrigal music.

Instruments

Creating music with instruments was not a new idea. However, many instruments were improved upon in the Renaissance period. The first violin was also made during the Renaissance, in the early 1500s. In addition to woodwind instruments like the recorder and bagpipe, some popular choices include:

- Hurdy Gurdy- This instrument had a similar shape to a violin. Instead of a bow, a small keyboard is used. Each key corresponds to a string. When the key is played, a wheel rubs against the string and makes a sound.

Hurdy Gurdy

- Lute- The lute is similar to a guitar but has a rounded back. People would pluck these strings to make music instead of strumming them.

Lute

- Harpsichord- This instrument is similar to a piano, but it is plucked instead of hit.

Harpsichord

- Percussion instruments- Tambourines and drums also became popular during the Renaissance. They were usually played in addition to other instruments.

Though the musical instruments were an integral part of entertainment, vocal music was more popular and commonly heard than instrumental music.

Dance

Dance was not as creative and free of a movement as it is today. There were two types of dances; country dances and court dances. Country dances allowed anyone to participate, while court dances were only performed by professional dancers. Court dances also required formal attire. Some of the most common dance moves included:

- Reverence- This was a 'greeting' when dancing. Dancers face each other as they slide their left foot back. Then, both knees are bent to bow to their partner.
- Pavane- This was intended for slow movements, so gowns and nice clothing could be displayed. The pavane was commonly the first dance of the courts.
- Saltarello- This upbeat dance required dancers to step forward three times, then hop.
- Italian Doppio- Also called the Italian Double, this step required dancers to take two long, elegant steps forward and then rise on their toes.
- Ballet was created during the Renaissance, too. It began in the courts of the nobles and eventually spread to France. It was most popular when Catherine De Medici ruled over the country.

Literature and Theatre

In the earlier days of the Renaissance, only men of wealthier families were usually educated. This limited the spread of ideas, as common people could not read them. However, literature became more digestible forms of entertainment, especially theatre. Putting on plays was common for entertainment, especially later in the Renaissance.

William Shakespeare

William Shakespeare

Even today, Shakespeare is regarded as one of the best writers of all-time. He is responsible for creating words that are used in the English language today (like bedazzled) and coined many idioms (like 'break the ice'). Even his plot devices were unique.

Shakespeare was born in 1564. Not much is known about Shakespeare's early life. After marrying at 18, he had three children with a woman named Anne Hathaway. Several years later, they ended up in London. Here, Shakespeare worked with an acting company, Lord Chamberlain's Men. Usually, there were about ten characters in a play. Young boys played female roles because women were prohibited from acting at that time. Not only did Shakespeare act, but he also wrote plays for the group. Some of his most popular works included *A Midsummer's Night Dream*, *Romeo and Juliet*, *The Taming of the Shrew*, and *Richard III*.

Lord Chamberlain's Men performed at the theatre, however, they did not own the land. When the owner, Giles Allen, decided to tear down the theatre, the company dismantled and relocated across the Thames River. Eventually, the Globe Theatre would be constructed. This was a monumental playhouse, being able to hold 3,000 audience members. Musicians made special effects noises, and a cannon fired blanks at critical moments in the play. Some of his later works included *Macbeth*, *Hamlet*, *King Lear*, and *Othello*.

Globe Theatre

Other Notable Writers

While Shakespeare was one of the most well-known Renaissance writers, several others deserve a notable mention for their contributions:

- Geoffrey Chaucer- Chaucer wrote *The Canterbury Tales*, which was a major source of inspiration for Shakespeare. It was also the first serious piece of literature written in English, which was considered a 'common' language at the time. Having it in English made it more available to the public.

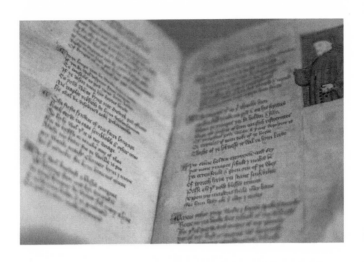

Manuscript of The Canterbury Tales by Geoffrey Chaucer from c. 1410, located in the British Library

- Niccolo Machiavelli- Machiavelli's major work is his book, *The Prince*, which was supposed to be a guidebook for rulers on how to behave. However, some historians argue it was actually a guidebook trying to convince the masses to rise up against the government. Niccolo di Bernardo dei Machiavelli is credited as one of the most important figures of political influence from the Renaissance. Machiavelli's book lay the foundation for how a political leader should behave. *The Prince* sent the message a true leader would be considered almost holy by the public, being someone that deserved to be followed. However, leaders must also be able to commit evil when it is necessary. This idea is one that would have an influence in the psychology field as well, as someone who is likely to do an evil act for personal gain is said to have a Machiavellian personality.

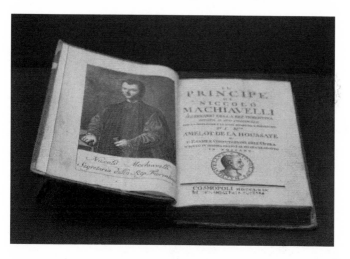

El Principe de Niccolo Machiavelli

- Dante Alighieri- *The Divine Comedy* is a poem that Dante wrote from his perspective of traveling through Hell. The poem has many religious themes and is very complex, especially for the modern day reader. Despite its complexity, *The Divine Comedy* stands out as one of the most beautiful works in literature. Many people of the time disagreed with Dante's critiques of Florentine politics, culture, and society, however, the themes can even be seen in modern day culture.

Statue of Dante Alighieri

- Miguel de Cervantes- *Don Quixote* is considered one of the first novels ever written. Cervantes lived during the Renaissance, but his influence was greater in Spain. He played a major role in what is known of the Spanish language, as his novel was the first of its kind. Though the book was published in 1605, its literary influence continues today.

Don Quixote and Sancho Panza monument with Cervantes

Entertainment from the Renaissance period is still around today. We can credit it for many of the instruments we have mastered. Additionally, many classical authors from the time wrote works so highly regarded that they are part of school curriculum today.

Chapter 4: Great Scientists and Discoveries During the Renaissance

With scientific discovery comes change. The end of the Medieval Times is often referred to as the Dark Ages, as people were not working toward learning more about their existences. People had been less interest in arts and the sciences and more interest in religion. However, the Renaissance brought about change. Many great scientists of the time can be credited for the ideas behind scientific exploration and the technologies that are available to us today.

Science in the Renaissance

There are many inventions today that were conceptualized or created during the Renaissance period. Even ideas like the scientific method were conceptualized and perfected, which is the basis of how we test theories and ideas today.

Leonardo da Vinci's Scientific Contributions

Don Quixote and Sancho Panza monument with Cervantes

While da Vinci is most known as being a great artist, he was considered an Italian polymath. Put simply, this meant that he was skilled in many areas. Reports of da Vinci state that in addition to being a great artist, he was also an architect, musician, writer, inventor, mathematician, and scientist.

Da Vinci's drawings are some of the most notable from the time. Many discoveries during the Renaissance would encourage later studies. Da Vinci pioneered the study of human anatomy and other scientific observation. Da Vinci, being a 'Renaissance man' who excelled in many areas of human excellence, proved that art and the sciences could be combined. For example, consider the way video game characters move around in a fake world. The artful design of the world and the characters add to gameplay and the experience, while the understanding of physics and the human body is used to help that character move through the world in a more engaging and realistic way.

Even though da Vinci would only be known for his art, he is responsible for conceptualizing many great ideas, including a calculator, the double-hull design of a boat, solar power, an armored vehicle, and a helicopter. However, the materials available during da Vinci's lifetime never let him bring these ideas to light.

Some of da Vinci's smaller inventions were used in manufacturing at the time, including a machine that tested the tensile strength of wire and an automated bobbin winder. Da Vinci is also known for his contributions in the fields of civil engineering, hydrodynamics, optics, and anatomy.

Francis Bacon and the Scientific Method

Francis Bacon

Francis Bacon was a highly regarded philosopher. However, he is also credited for his work with the scientific method. Unlike the accepted doctrines of Plato and Aristotle, Bacon emphasized the importance of experimentation and offering proof with theories. He believed that data should be gathered and analyzed to find a theory. Once a theory was chosen, scientists must find a way to experiment and test that theory. Bacon operated under the philosophy that by organizing and observing nature's truths, science could be used for the betterment of humanity. His ideas were rejected at first, especially by Lord Burghley (Bacon's uncle) and Queen Elizabeth. However, after publishing the first book of *Novum Organum Scientiarum* in 1620, Bacon found the respect of his peers.

Bacon is known for having said, 'knowledge is power.' This belief is something that has inspired many to seek out an understanding of ideas through science. He helped create the divide between religion and philosophy by using observation and deductive reasoning. Prior to Bacon, people had difficulty separating the ideas of philosophy from those of religion. Though both focus on goodness to a certain extent, this separation was critical in dividing church and state as well. This separation went on to influence the political structures of today as well, with the separation of the government from the church.

Francis Bacon's ideas taught the importance of human thought. Bacon taught different modes of inquiry and displayed how to ask questions and seek out a specific answer. Following these modes of inquiry is only natural, as humans have a curious nature. Without seeking an understanding of the world around us, we greatly limit our abilities and stifle ourselves in that area of creative thought.

Other Inventions of the Renaissance

- The Clock- The earliest clock was invented in the 1400s, and then, Galileo improved it after inventing the pendulum in 1581. The invention of the pendulum increased the clock's accuracy.
- Warfare- While the people of the Middle Ages relied on castles for protection and knights for warfare, the Renaissance saw the invention of muskets and cannons, which worked using gunpowder and changed how war was fought. Submarines were also invented during this time.

Cannon

- Barometer- In 1643, Evangelista Torricelli created the first working barometer. Inspired by Galileo, he noticed how air pressure changed the level of the water in a glass tube. The initial tube was 35-feet tall—so early experiments were conducted on a grand scale. He tested different liquids, finding that heavier liquids like mercury let atmospheric pressure be measured with a small tube.

- Italic Typeface- Italic style writing was invented in 1500 by Aldus Manutius and Francesco Griffo. Manutius owned a printing company. The style was first used on an illustrated title page of a collection of letters by Catherine of Siena. Italics are used to create *emphasis* today. Manutius' original goal was to save space in writing, which could cut paper costs, and to mimic cursive writing, an art form that was exclusively for the wealthy which, in turn, provided good business for his company with business.

- Robotic Knight- This remarkable design is another of da Vinci's. He may have designed and executed this 'robot' at a celebration at the home of Ludovico Sforza, the Duke of Milan. Da Vinci's design involved rigging a suit of armor with wheels, gears, and a pulley system. By operating the pulley, the suit of armor would animate. In 2002, da Vinci's design was tested and found to be successful.

- Anemometer- In 1450, Leon Battista Albertia designed the anemometer, a device to measure wind speed. The simple design measured the incline of a disk positioned perpendicular to the wind. Leonardo da Vinci and Robert Hooke would each take a turn improving this invention for a more accurate reading.

Modern day anemometer

- Scuba Diving Gear- Da Vinci designed this
  invention while in Venice, as water
  surrounded the island city. The design
  included a bell-shaped device and
  breathing tubes that sat above water, a
  protective face mask, a leather diving suit,
  and goggles. Though da Vinci did not try
  this out himself, it may have inspired the
  creation of successful scuba gear in the
  1940s. Jacquie Cozens built and
  successfully tested in 2003.

Discoveries in Astronomy

The science of the moon, planets, stars, and celestial bodies in outer space is known as astronomy. As people explored the world around them, they also looked beyond the planet they lived on. Prior to the Renaissance, people believed the Earth was the center of the world. Greek scientists like Ptolemy and Aristotle had theorized this idea many years before.

Nicolaus Copernicus

Statue of Nicolaus Copernicus

Nicolaus Copernicus is credited as the first to develop a heliocentric theory of the universe which places the sun as the center of the universe.

Even though this is what we know to be true today, most people laughed at this theory during the Renaissance.

Galileo Galilei

Statue of Galileo Galilei

Hans Lippershey created the first telescope in 1608. But at the time, the invention was more of a concept than had any practical use. The telescope could be used to see across far distances, but it was ineffective for studying astronomy. Galileo changed the design and improved the quality of the image produced by the lens, which let him study the planets. Among his discoveries were the moons of Jupiter, sunspots, the phases of Venus, and the crater-filled surface of the moon. Galileo even theorized that the moon reflected the sun's light rather than producing its own, which we know to be true today.

As Galileo studied the movement of the sun and those planets he could see, he agreed with Copernicus' earlier theory that the sun was the center of the universe. He explained his work in a famous paper. However, the Catholic Church disagreed with his ideas. As punishment for his 'crazy' theories, Galileo was put under house arrest.

Tycho Brahe and Johannes Kepler

Statue of Tycho Brahe

Brahe was another long-term astronomy enthusiast who studied the planets and stars, taking precise measurements and comparing their movements. Later in his life, he took on a German astronomer, Kepler, as an assistant. Together, their work proved Copernicus' heliocentric theory. Kepler also wrote three laws of planetary motion and charted the movement of various planets, proving that they moved in an ellipse rather than a circle.

Illustration of Johannes Kepler

Paracelsus and Medicine

Paracelsus

Swiss-native Theophrastus von Hohenheim, known simply as Paracelsus, was a scientist and botanist born near the end of the 15th century. He challenged medical practices of the time, noting that many treatments offered by medical practitioners actually made their patients worse. He is responsible for some of the earlier studies on medicines and chemicals that helped heal.

Paracelsus was also one of the first to look at the human diet and environment as possible sources of illness. This idea was a major stride in medicine.

Sir Isaac Newton

Illustration of Sir Isaac Newton

Newton was born toward the end of the Renaissance, so it is hard to argue whether he is a true Renaissance scientist or not. However, Newton was greatly influenced by the work of the Renaissance scientists who came before him. In his studies, he followed the work of Copernicus, Aristotle, Kepler, Galileo, and Descartes. At first, Newton was not interested in publishing his ideas. He did not begin recording them until friend and astronomer, Edmond Halley, urged him to share them with the world. When Newton wrote the *Philosophiae Naturalis Principia Mathematica* in 1687, Halley paid to have it published. In this book, Newton described the law of gravity and the three laws of motion.

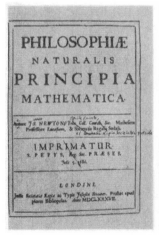

Isaac Newton's Philosophiæ Naturalis Principia Mathematica published 5 July 1687

These incredible discoveries are still used today. Some of his ideas and inventions include:

- Laws of Motion- The three laws of motion are fundamental physics laws, describing how atoms interact with their environment. These laws also laid the foundation for classical mechanics.
- Gravity- Theories on gravity finally explained how the sun could be the center of the universe and how the planets orbited around it. It is rumored that Newton got the idea after watching an apple fall from a tree.
- Reflecting Telescope- Though Galileo laid the foundation for astronomy, his invention was a refracting telescope. Newton, however, created a reflecting telescope that used mirrors to create the image. This use of mirrors made it more powerful than Galileo's model. Most major telescopes today use a reflection technique.
- Calculus- Newton's original name for what we know as calculus is 'fluxions.' This explains complex calculations used in science and advanced engineering.

The field of science advanced greatly in the Renaissance period. While many inventions have been redesigned, we can credit the initial ideas to

the scientists mentioned in this chapter, as well as
many others.

Chapter 5: Humanism, Education, and Important Figures of the Renaissance

Humanism took hold in 14th century Italy. Whereas the Dark Ages had lost focus of what it meant to be human, the principles of this movement promoted the idea of man as the center of his own universe. Humanism insisted that people embrace their own achievements, be it in the field of science, literature, education, or the classical arts.

The idea quickly spread. Johannes Gutenberg invented the Gutenberg printing press in 1450. Following that, it became common practice for great thinkers and humanist authors, including Francesco Petrarch and Giovanni Boccaccio, to write and print texts. The texts were distributed across Europe, greatly contributing to Greek and Roman culture and values.

19th Century Illustration of Gutenberg and His Press

The spread of humanism was a paradigm shift from the idea of a vengeful God. Though religion was not pushed aside entirely, humanism challenged the idea that man was not worth anything. It assigned value to human contribution to society. Humanism is akin to the liberal arts of today, encompassing those areas of human study like music, art, poetry, history, philosophy, and literature.

The revival of arts and humanism did not necessarily mean religion was less important. In fact, religion remained a critical part of the ideas behind philosophy. People still wanted to do things that were considered 'good.' However, they were in search of a happier existence.

Erasmus (Desiderius Erasmus)

Erasmus is considered the greatest scholar of the Northern Renaissance. His major contribution included the critical study of the history of the past, particularly the Church Fathers and the New Testament. Erasmus also analyzed classic writings. He criticized some methods of the past and encouraged new humanist approaches, pioneering reforms in the church.

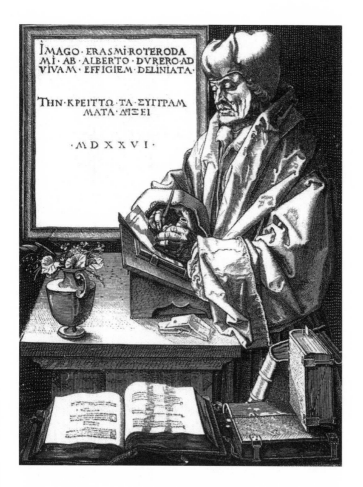

Portrait of Erasmus von Rotterdam, 1466-1536, drawn by Albrecht Dürer

Erasmus greatly valued education over religion. Like many other scholars, he doubted the idea of an immortal soul. He also played a critical role in understanding human nature. Erasmus believed

103

human nature could be molded, encouraging better attributes and discouraging those that were unsavory. He believed that through education, any type of change was possible.

One of his most well-known books is *Praise of Folly*. This book was rife with irony, as the scholar began questioning his own ability to spark change around him. He maintained that, "Even the wise man must play the fool if he wishes to beget a child."

Education During the Renaissance

Major shifts were happening in educational systems. In the Middle Ages, learners were attracted to theology, logic, and metaphysics. They wanted to understand how the world worked. Humanists were different in their learning desires. They sought education in schools that emphasized history and literature, working to improve thinking, writing, and speaking. Pier Paolo Vergerio (1370-1444) once said that the studies of the time were liberal because they were 'worthy of a free man.' Rather than a specific type of learning, schools emphasized the goal of developing character and preparing students for civic activity. Education combined ancient studies of the Greeks and Romans with more modern teachings from medieval times. The idea of doing what was good and practicing morality also aligned with the Christian values of the time, without being as extremist as the Middle Ages.

Many of the changes in education were brought about by the new ideas of humanism and the way it encouraged people to think for themselves. They were no longer living according to a rigid, unchangeable code but questioning the world around them. Through inquiry, people began to understand the world. This questioning led to many scientific, architectural, and other developments.

Francesco Petrarca and Education

Francesco Petrarca, or Petrarch, is credited with the revival of classical learning. Known as a poet of his time, Petrarch was among the first Italian writers that strayed from medieval learning or scholasticism. Scholasticism had the goal of reaching an understanding or truth. Language was not meant to inspire emotion or ask questions, but to provide certainty. The problem was that scholasticism eclipsed what was known as Augustinian tradition. Petrarch read Saint Augustine's works and learned more about the humanist branch of learning which focused on studying oneself. By looking and working inward, a person could guarantee his or her own salvation.

Through literature, music, and the arts, people could cultivate a special relationship with God. Traditional education focused on arithmetic, natural science, logic, and the study of divinity, but people considered these topics insignificant. While there was still a place in the sciences, one must also study philosophy and its application in the real world. Only by becoming a master of thought could one move on to a greater place in life.

Of course, some of Petrarch's ideas can be attributed to Dante's writing. Dante lived prior to the Renaissance, but people believe he predicted the coming revolt against the Christian church. Dante died before he saw the revolution, but Petrarch helped set his ideas in motion.

Rene Descartes

Illustration of Rene Descartes

Rene Descartes, born in France in 1596, was a scientist, mathematician, and philosopher, as well as one of the first to abandon traditional scholastic methods introduced by Aristotle. Descartes also introduced mind-body dualism, which is the existence of the mind and body as separate entities. This concept founded the basis for early psychology. Like Francis Bacon, Descartes also insisted on science and evidence rather than accepting theories as truth. He is responsible for the scientific technique of deductive reasoning, which he wrote about in his books *Discourse on Method* in 1637 and *Rules for the Direction of the Mind* in 1628 (though the latter was not published until 1701). Descartes' principles can be separated into four ideas:

- Do not accept anything as truth that you do not know as truth for yourself
- Always divide problems into their simplest parts
- Begin with simple and proceed to the complex while problem-solving
- Always recheck reasoning

Like many astronomers before him, Descartes believed the world was not the center of the universe. However, the Catholic Church was still suppressing this idea at the time, especially in Rome. After writing his book on this, *The World*,

Descartes learned Galileo was suppressed and retracted his book.

Discourse on Method was also monumental because it was an important philosophical work that was not written in Latin. Instead, Descartes wrote in French, which was widespread at the time. He believed this would make information available to all people, including women. *Discourse* also presented a moral code that all should follow when trying to find the truth.

Another major work by Descartes was *Meditation on First Philosophy, in Which Is Proved the Existence of God and the Immortality of the Soul.* This 1641 book included responses by philosophers of the time on various philosophical topics, including entries by Descartes himself. This feat was incredible at a time when differing ideas and restrictions from rulers and the church suppressed differences in philosophical thought.

Other Influential Figures of the Renaissance

Of course, while those with humanist principles had a significant impact in this area, many others had a great influence on the Renaissance period. Among those who deserve notable mentions are:

- King Henry VIII- King Henry VIII was a man of many talents. Like Leonardo da Vinci, he was often referred to as a 'Renaissance man.' He could speak four languages, had an attractive, confident appearance, was a musician and composer, a good horseman, and a strong fighter. His major role was separating the Roman Catholic Church from the Church of England, which undoubtedly encouraged the move away from a central religion.
- Martin Luther- Martin Luther challenged the ideas of the Catholic Church, especially the idea that people must pay heavily to get into Heaven. He also challenged the Pope's authority, stating that the Bible should be the final word on anything. His radical ideas sparked a reform, bringing forth Protestant Christianity.

Illustration of a portrait of Martin Luther

- Catherine de Medici- As a young girl, Catherine was captured to stop the Medici family from attacking a city-state. After convincing her captors that she wanted to

be a nun, she was allowed to live. Several
years later, she married the King of France
and rose to power as a queen. Later, her
sons would rule over Poland and France
and her daughter would rule as Queen of
Navarre.

Catherine de Medici

- Christopher Columbus- Though Columbus was not the first to discover America, he did play a major role in sparking new exploration through the Americas. Though he was trying to find a shorter route to Asia or the East Indies from Spain, he stumbled on the coastline of America.

Christopher Columbus Engraved Portrait, Circa 1490

- Vasco da Gama- This explorer played a major role in finding shorter trade routes. He traveled around Africa from Europe and arrived in India. This route was much shorter than ones previously used, strengthening trade between the territories.

Vasco da Gama

- Joan of Arc- The Renaissance was a period that heavily favored male figures. Men were educated and women were not. Typically, men had better opportunities except for those women who ruled as

115

monarchs. Joan of Arc was a French military leader and made great strides for women. However, she died young after being burned at the stake at 19.

Joan of Arc in battle

The Spirit of Humanism

Though people who study humanism often consider it an idea, humanism is truly a spirit of achieving human perfection through the expression of all those things humans can do that animals cannot. It is the value of human life. This idea, paired with expansion in the time and the exploration of new ideas, changed the future of humanity. It invited science, art, and learning while doing away with the restrictions of the church.

Conclusion: The Impact of the Renaissance Today

The Renaissance was a time of rebirth and brought new ideas to light, while still adapting to the changing times. Even today, the changes brought about by the Renaissance have shaped society. In fact, many historians say it had a major impact on the ideas and culture of western society today, especially in the Americas.

The Influence of Humanism

In the early days of America, humanism drew focus away from the church. As people focused on the ideas of humanism and the Renaissance, humans were assured of their importance in the world. Humanism encouraged scientific exploration and achieving human potential. Rather than focusing on religious ideals, humanism promoted the idea that all people were capable of achieving greatness by exercising their strengths. People turned away from the dominance of the church and found greater freedom of expression.

The Renaissance period also affected writers of the time. Prior to the Renaissance, the major focus was writing religious stories or those that focused on living a good, pious life. After the Renaissance, writers were more likely to focus on realism. With a more realistic version of life presented, people had a new platform to explore emotions and thoughts. The turn toward realism also affected the political climate.

The Renaissance also encouraged fiction writing. Before the Renaissance, stories were often based on gods, goddesses, and people who had achieved perfection because that was the way society embraced the human nature which left no room for human stories. Stories and plays would focus on 'real' characters with natural flaws. They were not perfect, but their imperfection made them more relatable to the general public.

How the Renaissance Affected the Freedom We Have Today

Finally, the Renaissance can be credited for influencing the way that American society experiences freedom. Prior to the Renaissance, people were more limited in their ideas. Religion had taken such a forefront that people would consider it first, which was evident in art and stories of the time, as well as the lack of scientific discovery during the Middle Ages. With the many great influencers of the Renaissance, however, the way that people thought changed. They were encouraged to explore their ideas, whether through art or scientific exploration. This freedom allowed the idea of what a human is and what a human can be to flourish, setting the tone for all the achievements in the liberal arts and sciences we know today.

More from Us

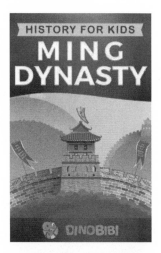